INDIAN CREEK
Arawak Site on Antigua, West Indies

1973 Excavation by Yale University and the
Antigua Archeological Society

by

Fred Olsen

Norman

University of Oklahoma Press

By Fred Olsen
On the Trail of the Arawaks (Norman, 1974)
Indian Creek: Arawak Site on Antigua, West Indies (Norman, 1974)

Library of Congress Cataloging in Publication Data

Olsen, Fred, 1891-
    Indian Creek.

    1. Indian Creek site, Antigua. I. Title
F2035.O5 1974   970.3   74-6018
ISBN 0-8061-1207-7
ISBN 0-8061-1208-5 (pbk.)

Copyright © 1974 by the University of Oklahoma Press, Publishing Division of the University. Manufactured in the U.S.A. First edition.

Contents

	page
Preface	v
Yale Excavation of the Indian Creek Site, 1973	3
Summary of Findings	47
January, 1974	52
Personnel	55

Dedication

To the many members of the Mill Reef Club who have so generously supported the work of the Antigua Archeological Society culminating in the 1973 excavation of the Indian Creek Arawak site; and to Dr. Irving Rouse who headed this Yale University excavation.

Preface

by Desmond Nicholson, president
Antigua Archeological Society

The inhabitants of Antigua, who produced the artifacts discussed in this book, were Arawaks, an Amerind people who came from Venezuela, probably by way of the Orinoco River and Trinidad, approximately two thousand years ago. They were skilled in pottery-making and agriculture—especially in the growing of manioc, which was their main source of food, supplemented, of course, by protein from fish and shell fish.

The 1973 excavation by Yale University has provided a copius store of Arawak artifacts that will be analyzed by Dr. Rouse in a technical document to be published perhaps about five years from now. In the meantime, I am glad to see this report by Fred Olsen, secretary-treasurer of the Antigua Archeological Society, which tells the story of the three months project at Indian Creek during the early summer of 1973.

In somewhat the same vein I would like to supplement Fred's account by citing some of my own findings about the Arawaks of Antigua—their association with their predecessors, the so-called Ciboney (named by the Arawaks Siba = stone, -eye = people, the stone people; likewise, Saba, the island to our north, is an Arawak name meaning rock or stone)—and also make reference to the Caribs who almost exterminated the Arawaks from the Lesser Antilles.

There is no firm evidence of Paleo Indian occupation of of the Lesser Antilles islands; these were the earliest hunting people who used flint and stone tools. Their remains have been found to be as early as 12,000 B.C. in Venezuela and about 5000 B.C. in Hispaniola. I am fostering the hope that they will also be found in the Lesser Antilles. Doubts have also been held about Meso Indians, no traces of whom had been found on these islands until Morellen Wilson and I discovered large flint blades in the Salt Lagoon and on Long Island, which turned out to be preceramic material of the Ciboney type of Amerinds. These appear to be first millennium B.C. artifacts. These finds were reported at the St. Lucia Congress in 1971 and since that disclosure a dozen or more preceramic sites have been studied in the Lesser Antilles.

Although the Caribs were encountered by the Spaniards, and the early journals make much of their cannibalistic practices, we have as yet found no archeological evidence of the Caribs occupying Antigua. It is our understanding that the Carib invasion of the Antilles occurred no earlier than A.D. 1200 and perhaps as late as A.D. 1400, based on Carib statements to Columbus that they had arrived "a little while ago."

With all this movement through the islands, it is natural that the Indians should have given names to each island, and sometimes we know two names, one Arawak and one Carib. Antigua was called Yaramaqui by the Arawaks and Waladli by the Caribs. The former name is mentioned by the son of Christopher Columbus in his account of his father's voyages. The Carib name comes from Father Breton's dictionary of 1660.

The meanings of these names are not exactly known, but I have enjoyed my search through early sources for possible interpretations. I feel strongly that Yaramaqui means "Dagger Tree Islands" since "Yaruma" was the Arawak name of a tree from which rafts were made, and "qui" means "place of" or "land." To this day local fishermen make rafts from the big flower stem of the century plant, or dagger plant as it is also called. Yaramaqui seems to be an appropriate name, for surely few islands in this part of the Caribbean bear as many dagger trees as does Antigua!

The Carib name Waladli could possibly mean "Oil Island," as a similar word in Father Breton's dictionary means "oil." The Caribs were not referring to the mineral oil, petroleum, but rather to the organic oils to be found in turtles and fish. The Caribs used these oils for lighting and medicinal purposes. The Caribs, who lived mainly in Dominica and Guadeloupe, made foraging expeditions to Antigua. One of the purposes of these visits could have been to collect oil, since Antigua has more extensive reefs than their home islands, and turtle and fish were probably easier to find among these reefs.

January 1974

INDIAN CREEK

Figure 1. *Aerial photo of Indian Creek 1970*

Yale Excavation of the Indian Creek Site, 1973

It was in the winter season of 1955-56 that the first evidence of Arawak occupation of Antigua was discovered. It had originated during a chance meeting between Robertson ("Happy") Ward, the architect and founder of the Mill Reef Club, and Henry Gross—whose skill as a water diviner was the subject of Kenneth Roberts' book, *Henry Gross and His Dowsing Rod*. Gross had indicated on a map of Antigua where water might be found, and upon further prodding by Happy, who asked if he could dowse for things other than water, had marked likely spots for Indian artifacts on the same map. Happy's son-in-law, Ogden Starr, digging for Indian relics, misread the map and dug the spots marked for water. However, by some piece of serendipity, Oggie did find ancient potsherds which Happy and I guessed could be Arawak material, and thus he merits credit for discovering the Arawaks on Antigua.

After we had indulged in a few weeks of enthusiastic digging at Mill Reef I became uneasy that we might be ruining an archeological site, and called on Professor Irving Rouse of Yale University for advice. Fortunately he was able to visit Antigua and quickly identified the artifacts as Arawak. He also gave us some practical lessons in proper digging techniques.

The Mill Reef site proved to be a small one, and when excavation was completed we turned to cataloguing our finds and installing them in an abandoned sugar mill which has become the Old Mill Museum. We also scouted the island in search of other Arawak sites and in the course of this pursuit came upon Indian Creek. But because the extent and location of the site as well as the quality of surface finds seemed to indicate an extremely important habitation, we decided not to excavate on our own, but to garner our resources until such time as we could secure professional cooperation and leadership—hopefully that of Dr. Rouse. That time came at last, after several years of appeals for funds in the annual issues of *The Mill Reef Diggers' Digest*.

The funds, accumulated by the Antigua Archeological Society, were matched by Dr. Rouse with a grant from the National Science Foundation. On May 29, 1973 Dr. Rouse began a full scale Yale excavation of the Indian Creek site. The site, covering more than twenty acres, is shown on an aerial photograph taken by Brad Endicott as Frank Shelden, geologist from Mill Reef, piloted his plane at a conveniently low altitude (Fig. 1). The upper road, running obliquely just above the tip of the wing at the bottom right of the picture, is roughly north to south. The land slopes eastward toward a narrow band of trees which marks the bed of Indian Creek, dry except at times of heavy rain. It is our guess that the creek very likely was navigable from the sea by Arawak canoes a thousand years ago, possibly as far as the habitation site.

In 1965, the ground was almost bare of vegetation (Fig. 2), due to seven years of drought, although traces of acacia shrubs could be seen, which today form a dense, almost impenetrable thorn thicket. A profusion of conch and other shells was visible over much of the area, giving evidence of ancient occupancy.

Figure 2. *Indian Creek site, 1965, after several years' drought*

On the site are several mounds—actually "kitchen middens"—one of which (seen as a semicircular light band in Figure 1) is about a thousand feet long, a hundred feet wide, and apparently six or more feet deep. From surface finds the mounds appeared to be habitation sites of varying age, suggesting the possibility of revealing cultural changes spreading over a thousand years of occupation. We were pleased to come across, in one spot, some early Arawak Saladoid sherds (Fig. 3) showing the characteristic white-on-red (W-O-R) painted decoration which reminded me of pottery we had found at Cedros in southwest Trinidad, and for which we had obtained a carbon 14 dating of about 200 B.C. I felt sure the Antigua W-O-R sherds would be several hundred years later, since we now believe the Arawaks left Cedros about A.D. 100, crossing the Gulf of Paria to Venezuela and probably moving a little later into the Lesser Antilles, perhaps from Carúpano on the Peninsula of Paria.

Figure 3.
Arawak Saladoid W-O-R sherds, surface finds

It is part of our objective to determine when the Arawaks arrived at Antigua, but in the meantime I am guessing about A.D. 300. This idea was supported when we picked up surface specimens of early conch zemies (Fig. 4) which resemble Guadeloupe

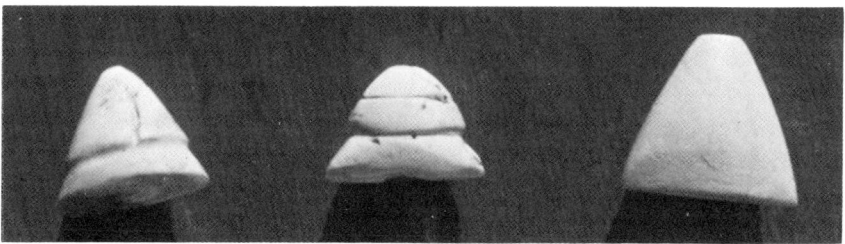

Figure 4. *Conch Zemies representing Arawak deity Yocahú*

zemies that Edgard Clèrc, of the Guadeloupe Historical and Archeological Society, had dated A.D. 220-240. I have described these zemies, in the 1970 *Mill Reef Diggers' Digest,* as representing the principal Arawak male deity, Yocahú.

We also found evidence of much earlier occupation of the site, although not by human beings. Beautiful specimens of petrified logs (Fig. 5) were scattered over the ground, proving that large trees once grew on this part of Antigua. Frank Shelden helped answer the question about the date of these fossil logs when he discovered part of a petrified forest at Corbison Point, Antigua (Fig. 6), with a three-foot diameter stump and long spreading roots in a deposit of lava. Presumably this lava had been ejected when a huge volcano "blew its top," leaving the six mile crater of which Boggy Peak (1,300 feet elevation) is now a stubby remnant. I pictured this ancient volcano as being possibly 5000 feet high, capable of enticing rain enough for such large trees. This lava with the petrified stump and roots underlies heavy beds of Oligocene limestone laid down in warm tropical seas about thirty million years ago (see *Mill Reef Diggers' Digest,* April 1972).

Figure 5. *Petrified log about thirty million years old*

Figure 6. *Petrified forest at Corbison Point*

In addition to the shells left by the Arawaks and the remnants of petrified logs, the ground of the Indian Creek site was also littered with stones—mostly debris from the surrounding limestone beds. One day as I walked over the field, a particular piece beckoned to me and I picked it up. It was a chunk of rock about the size of a baseball, roundish too, and

Figure 7a. *Lava ball*

brilliantly glossy. It looked almost artificially polished, but closer examination showed its surface to be an obsidian-like glass, denoting an igneous rock of volcanic origin. Slowly I realized that this ball (Fig. 7a) was another piece of evidence of the "big blow" before the Oligocene period. It had been molten magma spewed out of the depths of the earth, rounded by the strong surface tension of its viscous mass into a sort of hailstone as it flew through the air, solidifying into a lava ball that had captured a few seconds of the history of this geologic catastrophe of thirty million years ago. As one final and even briefer episode of this event, the flying missile had been just plastic enough when it hit the ground to entrap a few chips of rocky debris from some still earlier geologic formation.

Figure 7b. *Petrified log with burnt-in lava*

A second and perhaps even more significant find was a piece of petrified wood, showing clearly the solidified lava that had burned its way into a living tree (Fig. 7b). So I feel that this event of long ago has been quite fully documented.

Dr. Rouse planned a series of six trenches, each about twenty-five feet long by six feet wide and to a depth that would penetrate to ground sterile of human artifacts. These trenches were located in a long oval, beginning with the spot which had revealed the earliest artifacts on the surface, namely the W-O-R sherds and the conch zemies of Figures 3 and 4. The first task was the survey of the Indian Creek site by Dave Davis, a graduate student of Dr. Rouse. North-south and east-west lines (Fig. 8) were cut through the dense acacia thickets which had covered the land in recent years.

Figure 8. *North-south line through site*

Figure 9. *John Meade, foreman*

We had obtained as foreman of the working group a native Antiguan, John Meade (Fig. 9), a former senator from the English Harbour area of the island. John showed his diplomacy by employing as diggers five men who owned local property and would not only aid in protecting the site but would also be able from firsthand knowledge to dispel rumors that we were digging for gold or other treasure.

Trench 1 was laid out in four sections, each two meters square. Pits 1 and 3 were dug first (Fig. 10) in successive twenty-five-centimeter layers (about ten inches) with pick and shovel, relying on quick eyes to avoid damaging ceramic or shell artifacts. This permitted speedier excavation and also gave opportunity to dig pits 2 and 4 more carefully if the nature of the finds warranted so doing. Dr. Rouse instructed the men how the operations should be carried out, and personally searched the screens for artifacts (Fig. 11) as the loose dirt was sifted out by shaking. He selected every piece of pottery, bone, and flint, as well as shells, stones, or coral that gave any evidence of having been used by man. These were placed in shallow wooden trays, each bearing a label designating the trench, pit, and level at which the artifacts had been obtained.

Figure 10. *Beginning of trench 1*

Figure 11. *Dr. Rouse selecting artifacts from screen*

Figure 12. *Ben picking charcoal from pit*

He also gathered charcoal from the screens, the dirt going through them, and from the floor of the pit (Fig. 12).

Figure 13. *First mornings' yield of artifacts*

By noon of the first day there were two full trays of artifacts, one from each pit (Fig. 13). We could see some evidence of sherds with white-on-red decoration, but I was quite disappointed at the small quantity of this style of pottery.

There was, however, one piece of luck—an elegant pendant, carved skillfully from a conch shell. It looked like a highly stylized face with two eyes and a prominent nose (Fig. 14).

Figure 14. *Our first treasure*

11

On the first afternoon we had a visitor, Miss Florrie Drew; and I was expecting her. Almost ten years ago, during one of my early visits to Indian Creek, I had seen a native woman brandishing a cutlass while chasing some children. After they had dispersed she came toward me with her cutlass still at arm's length. I stood my ground and as she noticed my friendly smile, the fierce look left her eyes and she explained with indignation, "They were trespassin' on ma property," to which I responded, "Well, I guess I'm trespassing also. But this gives me the opportunity to ask your permission to be here. I'm looking for Indian relics like these," and I handed her some sherds I had just picked up. "I am Fred Olsen, and I live at Mill Reef." Instantly, with great dignity, but with her jaw pointing upward toward me, she said, "I am Miss F-L-O-R-E-A-N-C-E D-R-E-W [spelling it out for me] and I live at English Harbour." I shook her outstretched bony hand. She asked about the sherds and I told her they had been made by Arawak Indians perhaps a thousand or more years ago. I added that I would like to dig on her property and try to find more evidence about how the Indians had lived. She said I was welcome to do so. We have been friends ever since, and I can always count on seeing her because her cattle graze the land. I had written, telling her of the excavation that Yale would make on the land belonging to her and several other owners, under agreement made with the Antigua government.

As soon as she arrived she greeted me warmly and was glad to meet my daughter Liz. She obviously knew all the workers and two of them were amused when Miss Florrie stepped into the trench and showed them how to dig (Fig. 15).

Figure 15. *Miss Florrie shows how to dig*

Figure 16. *She picks artifacts from screen*

Figure 17. *Tries her hand at screening*

I knew she was seventy-three years old and had walked about four miles to reach the site, but I was amazed at her wiry strength and tenacity. As soon as the screening began she was intensely curious as to what was being picked out and was soon busy putting sherds and flints into the tray (Fig. 16). Later she tried her hand at shaking the screen (Fig. 17) but I noticed that Arthur Payne gently relieved her of the task when he saw the screen was a bit too heavy for her.

Figure 18. *W-O-R sherds from trench 1*

When pits 1 and 3 had been dug to sterile ground as judged by finding no more artifacts, and also by the fact that the soil was of a pristine yellow brown color without any of the gray-black discoloration characteristic of refuse from a habitation site, digging was begun on pits 2 and 4. The trench was completed a couple of days later and Dr. Rouse made a collection to illustrate all the types of artifacts found in trench 1. This collection would be exhibited at the Fifth International Congress due to assemble in Antigua during the last week in July. Although I was disappointed in the paucity of material recovered from this trench it did justify our selection of the spot as an early occupation site. There were a few W-O-R sherds (Fig. 18) but I was much more intrigued by the five Z-I-C sherds that had been recovered from the screen (Fig. 19).

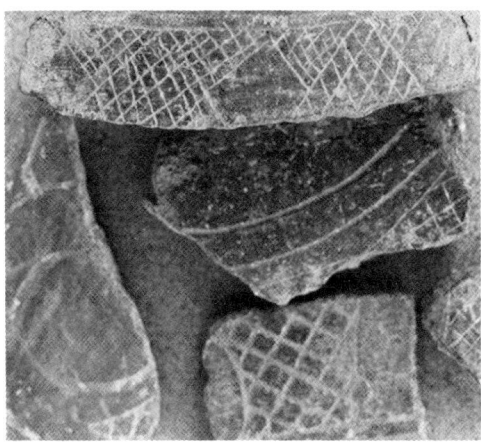

Figure 19. *Z-I-C sherds from trench 1*

This designation, Z-I-C, means "zoned-incised-crosshatched," and the incised crosshatching can be seen to be contained in separate zones of the design. These Z-I-C sherds are usually considered as a sort of time-marker, since they occur in the Lesser Antilles about A.D. 200-400. Both the W-O-R and the Z-I-C sherds are characteristic of what Dr. Rouse calls early Saladoid pottery made by Arawaks who were displaced from Saladero, their original home on the Orinoco (hence the name Saladoid), shortly after 1000 B.C. This migration of Saladoid Arawaks was caused by the appearance of a distinctly different Amerind tribe, called Barrancoid people after the town of Barrancas, near Saladero, where pottery quite different from the Saladoid was found. The relationship between the Saladoid and Barrancoid peoples has not yet been fully established and there is considerable disagreement among students of these cultures. It is my current opinion that the two tribes had quite separate origins. Possibly the Saladoids migrated from Ecuador since a similar style of thin, hard, painted pottery has been found in Valdivia on the coast not far from Guayaquil. Likewise, the Barrancoids may have come from the very early settlements in Colombia, where beautifully sculptured adorno handles, found in Puerto Hormiga near Cartagena, are strikingly like those made later at Barrancas on the Orinoco. I have been much impressed by the striking differences between the thin, hard, beautifully painted Saladoid pottery and the coarser, softer, but competently sculptured forms of Barrancoid ceramics. The painterly proclivities of the Saladoids and the sculptural concern of the Barrancoids remained distinguishing characteristics for the best part of two thousand years over a wide range of territory.

Figure 20. *Liz holds typical Barrancoid adorno*

Figure 21. *Barrancoid potters were sculptors*

A typical Barrancoid adorno (Figs. 20 and 21) was found in trench 1, but whether or not this is indicative of migration by Barrancoid potters from the Orinoco can not be determined at present. My guess is that it most likely represents the adoption by a Saladoid potter of the sculptural adorno features from Barrancoid pottery that had been obtained by trading. Also there were two nice shell spoons and a stone bead (Fig. 22).

Figure 22. *Two shell spoons and a bead*

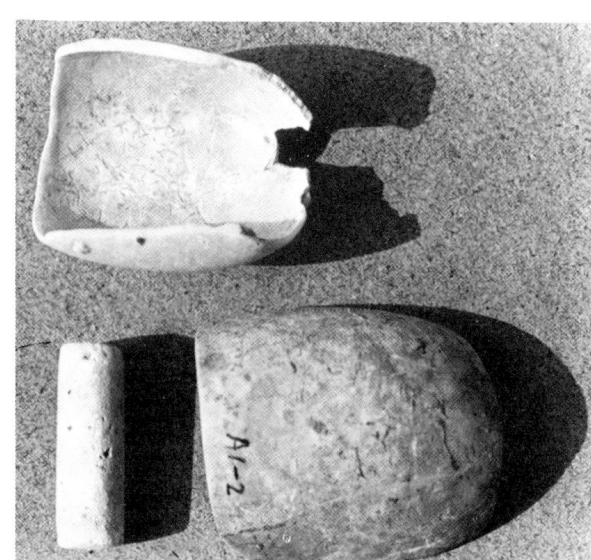

Figure 23. *Mandible of Arawak dog*

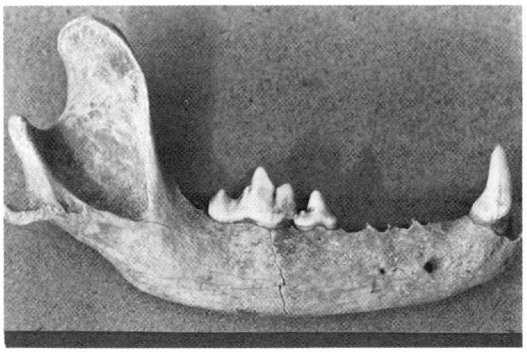

A well-preserved mandible of a dog—the Arawak hairless and barkless dog—was obtained (Fig. 23). The dog was bred for eating rather than for hunting in a gameless island.

Figure 24. *Desmond Nicholson, president of A.A.S.*

I close the episode of trench 1 with a picture of Desmond Nicholson, President of the A.A.S., whose energy is as indefatigable as his good humor is inexhaustible. He stands behind an acacia, one of those tiny shrubs shown on the barren land of Figure 2, now grown to a tree. His crown of thorns earns this picture (Fig. 24) the title "Superstar."

Trench 2, about fifty yards north of tench 1, was somewhat deeper but yielded another mediocre display of sherds. Consequently, I am illustrating this excavation more in terms of the characteristics of the diggers as we began to know them better and to develop a warm feeling for their individual personalities. Usually I visited them twice a day, at 10 a.m. and 3 p.m., to photograph the progress of the digging and to study the artifacts being unearthed. I brought them soft drinks, which proved quite welcome under the direct rays of a tropical sun. Although Cokes were the favorite, it was not always possible to secure enough of these on Antigua. The foreman, John Meade, showed his good will by seeing to it that his workers got their preferred beverage (Fig. 25) while he drank a strawberry soda (Fig. 26) which he liked no more than I do.

Figure 25. *Cokes for all*

Figure 26. *Except for John Meade's strawberry soda*

Another personal note is sounded in the picture of Arthur Payne (Fig. 27) carrying a heavy tray of sherds on his head during an uphill climb to the car that will carry the sherds for washing. His smile reveals not so much his gratification at the termination of a heavy day's work as his basic good humor.

Figure 27. *Heavy load carried lightly*

I have mentioned the poor yield of artifacts from trench 2. Specifically I am referring to the lack of Z-I-C sherds, whose absence suggested this was an occupational site later than trench 1. Also there was none of the early W-O-R pottery, but we did find examples of Saladoid pottery of a later vintage in which the

Figure 28. *Late Saladoid chevron design*

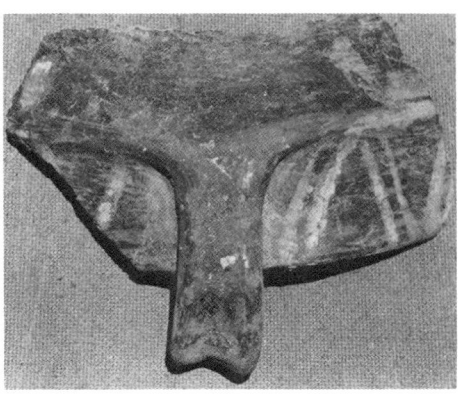

Figure 29. *Reinforced strap handle*

Figure 30. *Perhaps a barkless dog, trying to bark*

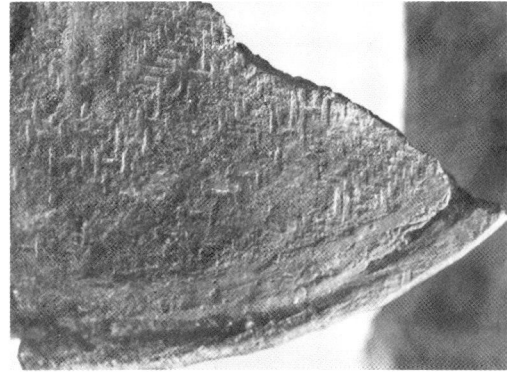

Figure 31. *Griddle sherd with impression of woven mat*

white bands, usually of a chevron pattern, were crudely painted on the underlying red surface (Fig. 28). There was, however, a very interesting large strap handle (Fig. 29), which is the first example I have seen of this technical achievement of strengthening the handle by use of spreading wing supports of clay worked onto the wall of the vessel.

Another artifact meriting attention is a unique ceramic adorno in the form of a head of an animal with wide open mouth (Fig. 30)—a splendid example of realistic sculpture, perhaps by some Barrancoid artist. Also of interest is a rare griddle sherd showing the impression of a woven mat on which the potter had placed the plastic slab of clay she was fashioning into a griddle (Fig. 31).

Trench 3 was started June 11 and was, in my eyes, another disappointing excavation, yielding an uninteresting group of sherds. Its bottom layer produced a few sherds of the late chevron patterns of crudely painted white bands, indicating the termination of the W-O-R style of pottery.

As usual, Ben scrutinized almost every screen load from the trench and studied each tray load of artifacts (Fig. 32). Trench 3 was also shallow—sterile ground being reached at a depth of about three feet. The lower part of the soil was extremely hard-packed, as indicated by the strenuous efforts of the digger (Fig. 33).

Figure 32. *Ben scrutinized almost every tray*

Figure 33. *Sometimes the digging is tough*

21

Figure 34. *Arthur listens to his donkey braying*

Each evening at five minutes to five, a loud braying was heard and Arthur Payne would recognize that his donkey was urging him to get ready to go home (Fig. 34). After announcing quitting time, Arthur's donkey waited patiently, taking the last few nibbles at the sparse grass (Fig. 35).

Figure 35. *Last nibbles before going home*

Figure 36. *a body stamp*

About the only artifact of interest from trench 3 was a body stamp that could be dipped into a vegetable dye (such as red from the rou-cou weed) and then used to stamp the design on the body. This discovery indicated the practice of rituals or dancing at this site (Fig. 36).

Trench 4 was at the most northerly point in the oval ring of excavations and at a lower part of the hill sloping down to the bed of Indian Creek. It was a bit deeper than the first three trenches, the bottom layer being at the four-foot level. However, once again the yield of artifacts was paltry and the small number of W-O-R sherds was of the later chevron style. Dr. Rouse seemed hopeful that this trench might yield pottery of a sufficiently later date to carry the occupation considerably beyond the span of the other trenches. He pointed out that the red ware was definitely well made, and showed good surface burnishing even if the decoration was scanty. Also the buff ware for culinary use was of similar technical competency. Since the yield of charcoal was plentiful at all layers we shall expect to establish good dates for the five layers of this excavation. In this connection I was much impressed by the care taken by our diggers in gathering the charcoal. Dr. Rouse had told them the importance of not contaminating the charcoal by picking it up with their fingers since the natural oils on the skin would contain carbonaceous matter of current date and might falsely reduce the antiquity of the bits of charred wood left from the ancient Arawak hearths. All samples were therefore lifted from the trench by forceps (Fig. 37), or by the trowel (Fig. 38). In the meantime I shall content myself by guessing that the absence of early W-O-R or Z-I-C sherds puts the lowest layer of trench 4 no earlier than A.D. 700, while the uppermost layer may be about A.D. 1000 to 1200, judging by the depth of the deposit in the midden.

All in all, these first four trenches were very disappointing to me. The artifacts we had encountered were skimpy in quantity and trivial in quality. Only the first had yielded any early Saldoid pottery, namely some Z-I-C and a few classic W-O-R

Figure 37. *Gathering charcoal with forceps*

Figure 38. *Using trowel to pick pieces of charcoal*

sherds. I had anticipated these items because trench 1 was located where we had found not only nice specimens of this early Saladoid material (Fig. 3), but also the type of conch zemies (Fig. 4) which I had concluded were the early embodiments of the cult hero Yocahú—the giver of manioc. Trench 1 was only a shallow pit, which could be interpreted either as the remains of an early Arawak occupancy of quite short duration, or the location of a fringe of a Saladoid village which started at trench 1, but did not show up in either trench 2 or 3 to any significant degree. This suggested a spreading of the village in some other direction—but in which direction? My hunch was that even in very early days, the choice real estate would have been lower down the hillside than trenches 1, 2, or 3, all of which were at a relatively high elavation. The lower locations would have been nearer the bed of Indian Creek, which, although currently dry for most of the year, is the lowest ground in the neighborhood and would have been the logical place to dig wells for drinking water. There was also the possibility that, a thousand or fifteen hundred years ago, Indian Creek might have been navigable to canoes returning from fishing expeditions.

I determined to test this idea and found it easy to enlist the interest of that intrepid navigator, Desmond Nicholson, who took us for a delightful sail in the beautiful ketch, Roxana (Fig. 39). from English Harbour eastward past the Pillars of Hercules (Fig. 40).

Figure 39.   *Desmond skippers ketch Roxanna to Indian Creek*

Figure 40.   *Pillars of Hercules—entrance to English Harbour*

We sailed along the south shore of Antigua to Indian Creek. Actually, there are two bays that form the opening to Indian Creek, the entrance to the outer bay being readily recognizable from the sea by the rocky headland, Standfast Point (Fig. 41). This promontory sticks out into the Atlantic Ocean, roughly forming a sort of counterpoint to Shirley Heights, which even from quite a distance out to sea identifies the location of English Harbour.

Figure 41. *Standfast Rock guards Indian Creek*

Figure 42. *Turk's Head Hill*

The outer bay of Indian Creek is a spacious harbor and affords a quiet water protection from the ocean swells. We sailed around its coastline admiring such scenic spots as Turk's Head Hill (Fig. 42) with its spectacular "army" of Turk's Head Cactus looking as if marching down the hill to repulse all invaders. The illusion of soldiers is enhanced by the stalwart barrel shape of the cactus, bristling with spines and topped by a gay red head.

It was such a pleasant place that we anchored off a little cove (Fig. 43) for a swim and lunch.

Figure 43. *Outer Bay of Indian Creek*

At the north end of the bay is the narrow entrance to the inner bay (Fig. 44) with its guardian rock.

Figure 44. *Entrance to Inner Bay*

Along the shore of this still more sheltered bay is low lying land rich in mangrove, with an occasional fine cinnamon tree of much darker and shinier leafage. It is at the northern end of this inner bay that the entrance of Indian Creek is found (Fig. 45), but it is not now navigable beyond the junction of the two hills.

Figure 45. *Indian Creek begins between the two hills*

It is not at all unlikely that, fifteen hundred years ago, this rising south coast of the island might have been low enough to permit the Arawaks to paddle canoes with their catch of fish, turtle or even manatee right up to the village represented by the midden mounds we were digging. I had no difficulty in picturing the fishermen returning to their homesite, not only glad of the smooth safety of these two entrance bays but very likely sensitive to the physical beauty of the sloping cliffs. I was reminded of Happy Ward's comment that when searching for an ancient Arawak site, first pick out the most attractive real estate. This pleasant Sunday cruise into Indian Creek territory had convinced me that very likely this had been a highly attractive spot for a great many years. I just couldn't help wondering if we would ever obtain factual evidence that this had been as great a site as I had pictured it, or if I would have to face the chagrin of having brought the Yale scholar, Dr. Rouse, to a mediocre site. We still had other mounds to explore, some of them apparently much bigger than anything encountered in trenches 1, 2, 3 and 4. Actually Ben had moved down the hill on Wednesday, June 20, to start the excavation of trench 5 (Fig. 46), and by Friday the men were digging in level 2 when a leg and foot of a figurine appeared (Fig. 47). The ankle was prominently sculptured and the white band below the knee reminded me of the fashion I had encountered in Surinam where only a chieftain was allowed to wear such a leg band. Perhaps this figurine represented a chieftain, or more likely a deity that was given the same kind of leg band as a status symbol. Possibly other parts of the figure would show up in the neighboring pits. We were looking forward eagerly to Monday morning to find more of the piece. But, alas, a bitter calamity occurred during the weekend. Dr. Rouse suffered a heart attack and was promptly taken by ambulance to the Holberton Hospital in St. John's, under the care of Dr. Luther Wynter, our much respected physician, who had been decorated by the Queen for his service to Antigua. Hoping that he might be well enough to resume charge of the excavation, we stopped the digging for two days; but he was held at the hospital for five weeks.

Figure 46. *Trench 5 Ben's last day at site*

Figure 47. *Leg of figurine, trench 5*

During those two days I asked John Meade and his men to help me explore the so-called ball court which I had found several years earlier. In March 1967, while taking a group of visitors to see the Indian Creek site, I had noticed a long pointed stone lying partly buried in the earth, which suggested to me a ball-court marker similar to those I had seen in Puerto Rico. It had been only a matter of minutes for the group to find three other stones which, when raised to a vertical position, marked the corners of a rectangle. The site was photographed (Fig. 48) and the four stones laid carefully in the holes from which they had been raised, in the hope of preserving the site until the time that Yale could make the excavation. I have been subjected to a goodly amount of razzing from my friends about this ball court. "Four stones could be selected from many spots that would form a rectangle," they said. I admitted that these four stones did not prove the site to be a ball court, but added that in my judgment it would be proved by the finding of only one fragment of a stone belt which the Arawak players used to wear.

Figure 48. *"Ball Court," March 1967*

Broken belts have been encountered frequently in Puerto Rico and I have three fragments in my collection (Fig. 49). Moreover, as several people pointed out, the view generally held is that the Arawak ball game, as evidenced by the thirty-four ball courts in Puerto Rico, was derived from Mexico, diffusing from Yucatan eastward to Hispaniola and finally to Puerto Rico. The great court at Chichén Itzá in Yucatán, with its stone rings tenoned into the walls thirty feet high and with temples at various parts of the court, is dated about A.D. 1200. The feeling is that the Puerto Rican courts should be perhaps A.D. 1250 or 1300 and recent carbon 14 dates support this. No ball courts have been found south of the Virgin Islands, and I have often heard the comment that no ball courts are likely to be found in the Lesser Antilles, since diffusion from Yucatán would be too late to reach these islands before the Caribs came.

My basic objection to this view has been that I find it difficult to believe that anyone could bring the quite complicated concept of the ball game from Yucatán to Puerto Rico without some suggestion of the masonry walls that dominate Chichén Itzá.

I have seen no example where any Arawak has ever placed one stone on top of another to build a wall.

My picture has long been similar to that of Theodore Stern, namely that the rubber ball probably originated where rubber was found, for example along the Amazonian tributaries, moving as a trade object—the magic bouncing ball—up the Orinoco and north through the islands of the Antilles. Also it could have travelled to Honduras, Guatemala and Mexico, where there are many ball courts, by a parallel route along the west of the Gulf of Mexico.

With no ball court in the Lesser Antilles, this remained an unsubstantiated hypothesis. For ten years I had looked for traces of ball courts in Antigua; and so, on June 26, 1973, we searched the Indian Creek area for the "ball court" I had found in 1967.

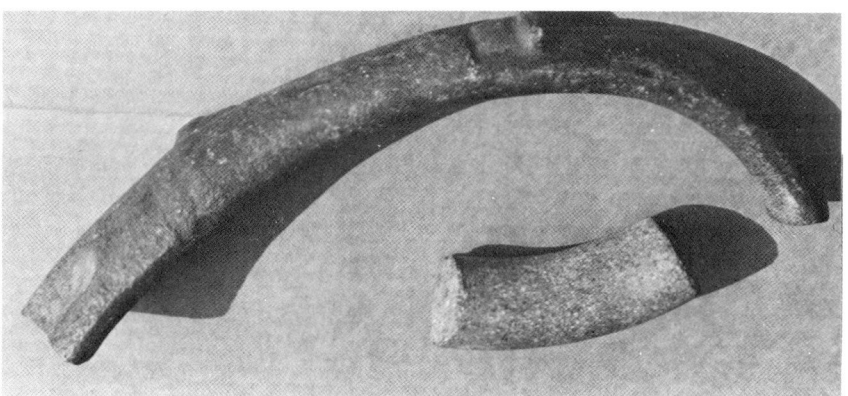

Figure 49. *Ball belt fragments, Puerto Rico*

Two of the original corner stones were located (Fig. 50). John Meade and the five workmen said they were not surprised that the other two stones were missing, since they were of just the size used for tethering cattle, allowing them some wandering in their search for food. Presumably donkeys or cows had sought relief from the hot sun and dragged the missing stones to a nearby shade. We hope to find them soon.

Figure 50. *"Ball Court" June 1973*

I showed the workmen an Arawak ball belt and my granddaughter, Robin, modeled the belt to show how it was worn (Fig. 51). Recently Desmond Nicholson had shown me a small cylinder of stone, whose ends were clearly ancient breaks, but for which he could think of no probable use. I recognized immediately that it was just like the fragments of ball belts I had obtained in Puerto Rico. He had picked it up "somewhere" on the surface of the Indian Creek site. To my thinking, the discovery of this fragment greatly increased the probability of the existence of a local ball court, but we needed to find a specimen "in situ."

Figure 51.
Robin models
Arawak ball belt

In mid-July 1973, a group of government officials were making their first visit to the site being excavated by Yale University. One of them was Basil Peters, minister for education and culture, under whose sanction the excavation was being conducted. About five minutes before the group reached the ball court site one of the workers handed me, from a low layer of trench 5 (Fig. 52), an oval piece of stone—obviously a ball belt fragment.

Figure 52.
A Ball belt fragment
is found in
trench 5, layer 5

33

Figure 53. *Ball belt fragments from Indian Creek*

It was made of the local "greenstone" from nearby hills (Fig. 53.)

This dramatic find made a definite impression on the visitors and a few minutes later Sydney Prince, minister of public works, came to me with a larger fragment he had picked up on the surface about forty yards from the ball court site. I recognized it as a broken piece of a "massive" ball belt (Fig. 53), which would probably weigh about forty pounds and be worn by a back-field player.

An important feature is that the greenstone fragment came from the fifth layer (about fifty inches deep) of trench 5. This layer had produced a mass of early Saladoid pottery—the fine, hard, white-on-red material—that could be as early as A.D. 500. This fragment furnishes evidence that the ball game was played in Antigua hundreds of years earlier than the date attributed to the Puerto Rico courts. It also suggests that the migration of the game was not eastward from Yucatan but probably northward through the Lesser Antilles.

During the last two weeks in July 1973, three more ball-belt fragments were found on the Indian Creek site, bringing the total to six specimens (Fig. 53).

At the Fourth International Congress at St. Lucia in July 1971 I had reported the finding on Antigua, by Desmond Nicholson and Morellen Wilson, of two preceramic sites with Meso-Indian flint and ground stone tools. This presumably stimulated the discovery of a dozen similar sites elsewhere in the Lesser Antilles. I am now predicting that the announcement to the fifth congress, held in Antigua in July 1973, of the finding of the Antigua ball court will very likely be followed by ball courts showing up in other islands of the Lesser Antilles.

By Wednesday, June 27, we had learned that Dr. Rouse would not be coming back to the site. The doctors were hoping that in a month or so he would be well enough to fly back to his home in New Haven. And this is precisely what happened. At the Hospital he was allowed no visitors other than his wife, and it was almost five weeks before I was able to see him and then only for five minutes.

Desmond Nicholson and I decided to continue the excavation just as Dr. Rouse had planned it, and it quickly became evident that Ben had taught John Meade and the five workmen so meticulously that they did a splendid job on their own, and kept the work on schedule. On the second day's digging both the quantity and quality of the artifacts changed dramatically. The pits of trench 5 suddenly became rich in the very same style of pottery that had been so discouragingly scarce. There had been *no* W-O-R sherds in levels 1 and 2 of trench 5, but there were fourteen pieces in level 3, and as the digging continued the flow of W-O-R material doubled in level 4 (Fig. 54). This condi-

Figure 54.   *Trench 5 rich in W-O-R sherds*

tion was maintained in level 5 and our first Z-I-C sherds appeared since the digging of trench 1. These Z-I-C sherds told us that we were definitely in the early occupation period. In the lowest layer, level 6, the W-O-R pottery was the dominant style.

Our good luck continued. The zemies that had been so scarce in trenches 1 to 4 showed up significantly in trench 5. In layer 4, forty inches deep, a well carved conch zemi (Fig. 55a) was found. Then in layer 5 (where the ball-belt fragment occurred) a very simple conch zemi (Fig. 55b) with well cut flat base appeared. No working of the sides of the conch was visible. So evidently we had found what I have previously designated as a "proto-zemi." A foot or so lower down, in layer 6, came a second proto-zemi (Fig. 55c), just a plain uncarved prong but with a flat base. The lower part of Figure 55 shows the flattened bases of the zemies.

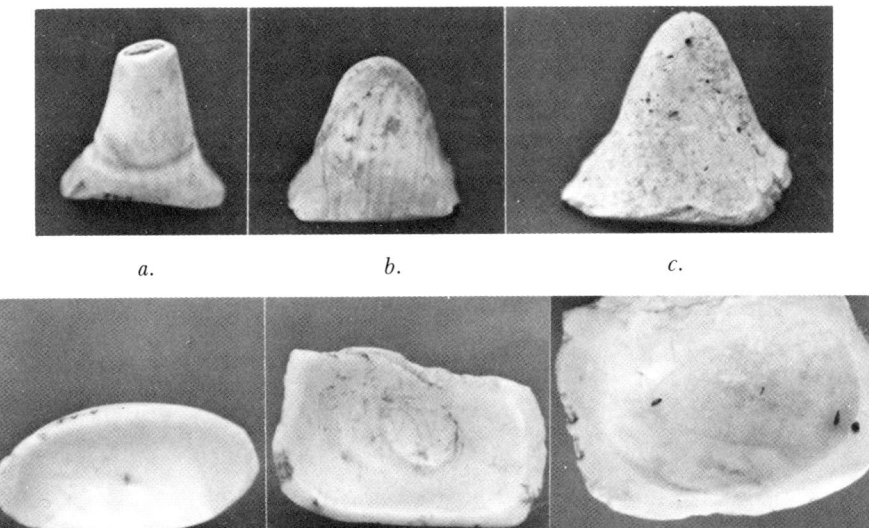

a. b. c.

Figure 55. *Early conch zemies depicting volcano where Yocahú dwelt— a: well-carved, layer 4, A.D. 860. b: "proto-zemi," a simple conch prong layer 5, A.D. 582. c: "proto-zemi" layer 6, A.D. 471. Base of zemies shown in lower part of picture.*

These were important finds, since they furnished evidence supporting my hypothesis of the evolution of Arawak religion— the cult of Yocahú. Briefly, this is that the Saladoid Arawaks, during their life on the prairies of the Orinoco, probably had a cult hero, Yocahú, the giver of manioc, but without any physical embodiment thereof, since no zemies are found on the mainland (see *Mill Reef Diggers' Digest*, 1970).

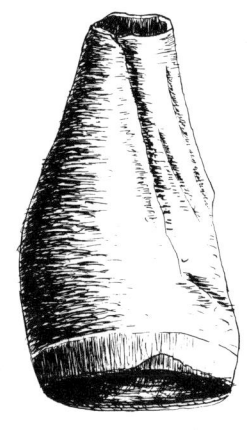

Figure 56. *Earliest "proto-zemi," Guadeloupe, A.D. 220*

Indeed, no such embodiment occurred during the first hundred years of occupation of the Lesser Antilles—the bottom layer of Morel I at Guadeloupe contains no zemi. The earliest known zemi is the conch cone found there by Edgard Clèrc in the bottom layer of Morel 2 (Fig. 56), dated A.D. 220. It is a simple prong of a conch shell.

My interpretation of this phenomenon is that some esthetically sensitive shaman, having witnessed an eruption of Mt. Soufrière in Guadeloupe, noticed the resemblance between the silhouette of the prongs of a conch and the skyline of volcanoes on the island of Basse Terre (Fig. 57). He conceived the idea that cutting off the prong of a conch, and smoothing its base so that the conch could stand upright, would give him a replica of the volcano in which he believed the Arawak god Yocahú resided. I

Figure 57. *Silhouette of conch shell prongs resembles skyline of Basse Terre's volcanoes.*

have designated this first simple conch as the "prototype" zemi, since, for the next three hundred years *all* the zemies at the Guadeloupe site were made of conch, although most of them were carved into smooth conical shapes, and some were incised with elaborate decoration. It was not until A.D. 575 that the first stone zemi occurred at the Morel site. From that time on, the size and complexity of the carved stone zemies increased steadily.

Naturally, I had wondered if this proposed evolution of the zemi had taken place earlier on the lush island of Guadeloupe, where a much larger Arawak population could exist, rather than on the tiny sparse island of Antigua. We had encountered no Mill Reef middens as deep as Morel 2, but now at Indian Creek the middens were much more extensive and much richer than at Mill Reef. The proto-zemies we had just found in layers 5 and 6 of trench 5 were as simple in form as the earliest one from Guadeloupe (compare Figs. 55 and 56).

Thus once more we have evidence of the early stages in the evolution of the Yocahú zemi. Recently (September 1973) carbon 14 results have been obtained from these three bottom layers of trench 5 yielding dates of A.D. 477, 582, and 860 (With a plus or minus of 85 years), so the Antigua zemies are somewhat later than the corresponding forms at Guadeloupe.

Even in the later stone zemies of A.D. 1400 from Puerto Rico, which show the human head of Yocahú, the characteristic volcanic cone of the earliest conch zemies is retained in the pointed hump of the back. The evolution of this sculptured form of the volcanic cone is thus traceable for about a thousand years. The coming of the Caribs is perhaps responsible for the broken condition of stone zemies found in late occupation layers in Guadeloupe and Antigua, possibly also for the absence of zemies in the topmost layers of some of the excavations in Guadeloupe and Antigua.

Apparently the Christian-Judaic concept of God making man in His own image was somewhat changed by the Arawaks who created their main god, Yocahú, in the form of the ubiquitous volcano in their newly found island paradise, even though in late forms Yocahú takes on anthropomorphic head and feet, yet the volcanic cone remains.

Whereas I was delighted to see all this fine material pouring out of the earth, I could not help realizing how disappointing it was that Dr. Rouse had been within one day's excavating of seeing the richness of the Indian Creek site that had stingily withheld its beautiful artifacts for so long.

Figure 58. *Trench 6 yields W-O-R sherd in top layer*

As soon as sterile ground was reached in the bottom of the sixth layer of trench 5 (at the five-foot depth) the site of trench 6 as previously selected by Dr. Rouse was staked out and digging commenced (Fig. 58). Even among the first few shovelfulls it was clear that this too was going to be a rich trench because a fine specimen of the classic W-O-R appeared (Fig. 59), hinting that a richer store of this type might be expected in the lower layers.

Figure 59. *Classic W-O-R sherd in layer 1 of trench 6*

This was substantiated by a steady increase in the quantity of Saladoid sherds (Fig. 60). These fine specimens, however, were merely an introduction to thirty lush W-O-R sherds found in level 5, some of them among the finest I have ever seen (Fig. 61).

Figure 60. *W-O-R sherds abundant throughout trench 6*

Figure 61. *Large W-O-R sherds from trench 6*

In the excitement of showing off these beautiful examples of Saladoid Arawak pottery I am cognizant that I have failed to introduce one of the hardest working groups, the sherd washers (Fig. 62). These important ladies moved literally from pillar to post, seeking room for their plastic basins with their heavy loads of potsherds and washing water, and for large flat spaces where the washed sherds could be spread to be dried, sorted, bagged, and labelled for storage, or shipment to Yale for study before being returned to Antigua for exhibition. Finally the washing crew was installed in the N.A.S.A. tracking station, built for the Apollo missions. Here the conditions were commodious and the work went along smoothly, keeping pace with the digging crew. It is the hope of the Antigua minister of education and culture that this fine building, which was given to the Antigua government by the United States, will eventually be developed into a cultural center with museum facilities for protecting and displaying the archeological and other historical material belonging to the Antigua National Trust.

Figure 62. *The washer ladies — Left to right: Florence Drew, Iris Hunt, Elizabeth Kyburg, Mildred Thomas*

From level 5 the supply of W-O-R sherds became still more numerous and elaborate. About a hundred were obtained, some of them quite large and handsome (Fig. 63), giving us an insight into the esthetic and technical competence of the potters who produced such graceful flared or bell-shaped thin-walled vessels, some with polychrome (Fig. 64) and baroque patterns of decoration.

Figure 63. *Graceful, flared, bell-shaped W-O-R vessel*

Figure 64. *W-O-R design above polychrome*

Figure 65.
Barrancoid type adorno with moray eel decorating the ear

It was in this rich melange that we came across one of the most elegantly sculptured pot handles—a highly glazed adorno showing what is probably a moray eel (Fig. 65), perhaps the most feared of all the denizens of the coral reefs. Also in the lower part of trench 6 were several incense burners. We had not previously encountered any on Antigua, although I had seen some at the Guadeloupe and St. Lucia sites. These were cylindrical vessels with a lid having a hole through which the incense vapor escaped (Fig. 66).

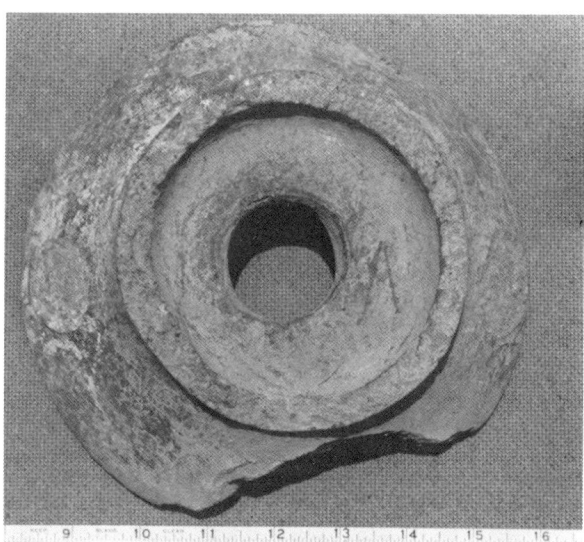

Figure 66.
Incense pot

Also prevalent were large strap handles for culinary vessels (Fig. 67). One obtained the impression of residents with a wide range of interests and with the competency and means to provide for them.

Figure 67. *Well-made handles for utility pots*

This wealth and diversity of material continued in level 6 (five feet deep in trench 6). The earliness of this layer was emphasized by the number of Z-I-C sherds, including the finest of the type I have seen anywhere (Fig. 68) with elaborate polished nubbins surrounded by crosshatching.

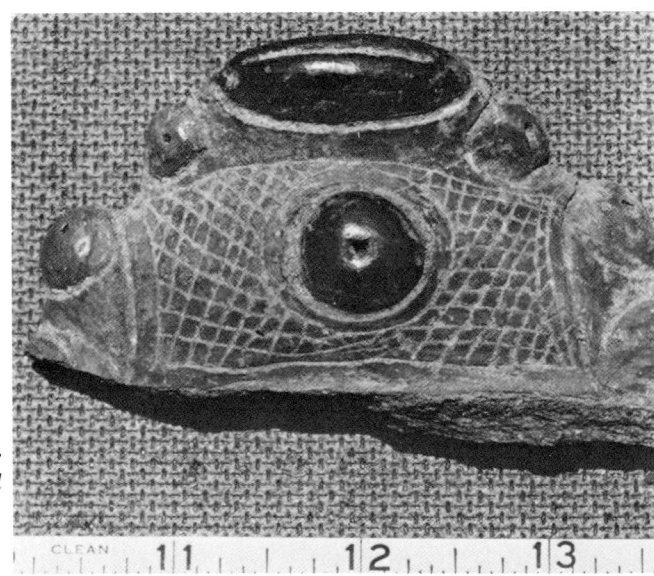

Figure 68. *Elaborate Z-I-C sherd*

When the trench was completed, we noticed that the stratigraphic layers which had yielded such a copious supply of splendid artifacts were dipping rather sharply to the east. Desmond and I therefore decided to continue the plan made by Dr. Rouse, believing that if Ben had been present he would most likely have been just as eager as we were to extend the trench downhill. Consequently a long base trench was dug, twelve meters long by two wide, in six separate pits—each two meters square, to form an inverted T with trench 6.

The decision was a profitable one, judged by the quantity of fine quality artifacts yielded by the new trench. We finished our digging with a flourish, and I like to describe it in this way. After digging for nine weeks without finding a single whole pot, we dug one day more and found three complete vessels (Fig. 69).

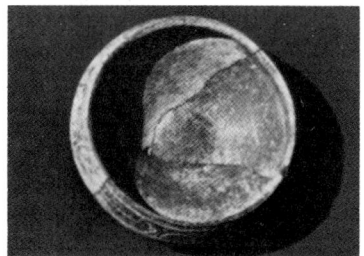
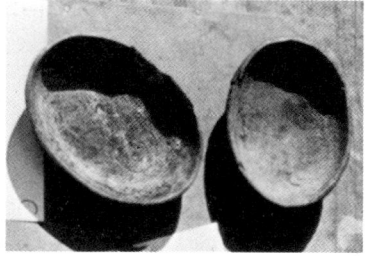

Figure 69. *Three complete pots found on last day's digging*

Figure 70.
Shell ornaments

Among these pots were some beautiful shell ornaments (Fig. 70). They appear to be too delicate to have been part of a necklace and suggest they might have been sewn on a cloth garment although no evidence of woven cloth has been discovered.

There was one elegantly carved shell pendant (Fig. 71) over which I have puzzled considerably. I am suggesting that it represents the choicest of Arawak foods, a manatee (sea-cow), as indicated by the characteristic broad shovel-shaped snout and the sweeping dolphinlike curve of the body.

Figure 71. *Shell carved as manatee*

Our digging was terminated by the arrival of some sixty-five archeologists to attend the Fifth International Congress for the Study of Pre-Columbian Cultures in the Lesser Antilles. This society had been inaugurated in 1960 when the first congress was held in Martinique. Subsequent meetings had taken place in Barbados, Grenada and St. Lucia and now it was Antigua's turn. In the course of a busy week of morning and afternoon lectures, the group took time to visit the Indian Creek site and the preceramic sites at Flinty Bay and Jolly Beach. Also they examined the exhibition of artifacts from each of the trenches as displayed in the N.A.S.A. tracking station. A brief visit was made to Mill Reef to see the Arawak artifacts at the Old Mill Museum.

Summary of Findings

Obviously we must await the interpretation by Dr. Rouse of the data from the summer's excavation, but I feel justified in stating that, seventeen years after our discovery of Arawak occupation of Antigua, this Indian Creek site has been shown to be worthy of being rated as a national monument and of being protected as such by the Antigua National Trust. I have urged the ministers of the Antigua government to establish regulations that will limit any future excavation to about 2 percent of the site, mainly to preserve it for future generations of Antiguans to explore, but also with the conviction that new archeological techniques will undoubtedly be developed which could reveal valuable information not now available to us.

Among those attending the congress was Ogden Starr. His son Michael, who was only three years old when his father discovered Arawak potsherds at Mill Reef, flew over Indian Creek this summer at the age of nineteen and took some fine aerial photographs. I am glad of the opportunity to reproduce three of these. Michael's view (Fig. 72) looks down the whole area from the paved highway (lower right corner) leading to the N.A.S.A. Apollo tracking station to the outer and inner entrance bays of Indian Creek in the south.

The bed of Indian Creek is revealed by the band of green trees (d) (Fig. 73) which wends its way (upward through the center of the picture) to its estuary at the inner bay (b). The eastern branch of the road after crossing the creek bed rises rapidly along the hilly ridge leading to the home site of Ralph Camacho (e) of the Antigua Department of Fisheries. His house (shown as a white dash in Figure 72) looks down the steep cliff into the outer bay (a). In the middle third of the picture the roads on each side of the creek are roughly parallel, and the ridges on which they run form the edges of a trough which carries the sea breezes to the long midden on which lie both trenches 5 and 6. These are seen as the two easterly trenches in the ring of excavations shown.

Figure 72. *Aerial view looking South down Indian Creek*

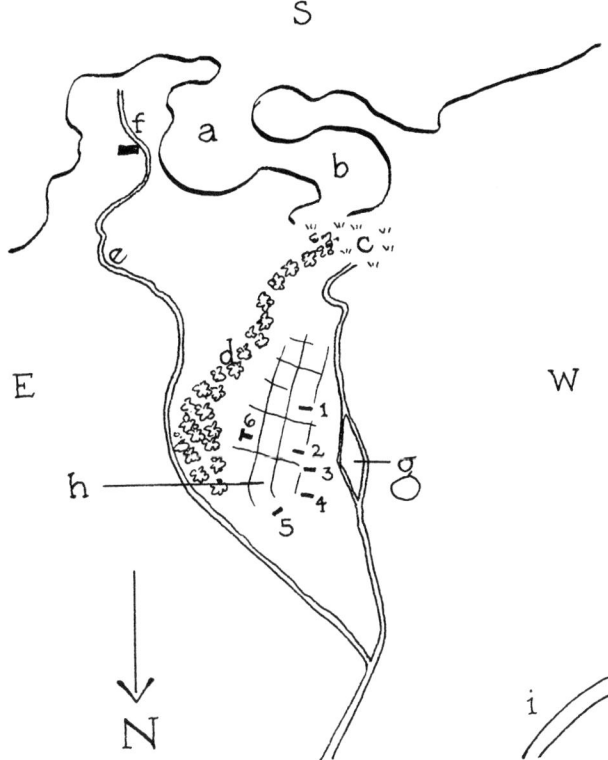

Figure 73. *Map of Fig. 72*

The north-south road skirts the high-lying western side of the excavation site. To the left of the narrow diamond shape (g) there lies what seems to be a faint grid of lines which is the area where the six trenches were dug. These are shown in the photograph as a circular pattern. I am frankly puzzled by this grid, which has the appearance of a village site of crisscrossing streets. We have no Antigua record of any such village during historic times, nor have any traces of modern artifacts been found there. However, I am by no means prepared to suggest that the grid relates to any orderly arrangement of Arawak house sites. I remember that six years ago there was a ploughed field of cotton here, but the rows ran at right angles to these roughly north-south prominent lines. Closer examination of the grid pattern reveals that there is only one clear-cut cross line, and this is undoubtedly the east-west line (shown in Figure 8), which we cut as a base line from which to identify the position of the trenches. Although I have no definite explanation of the grid I

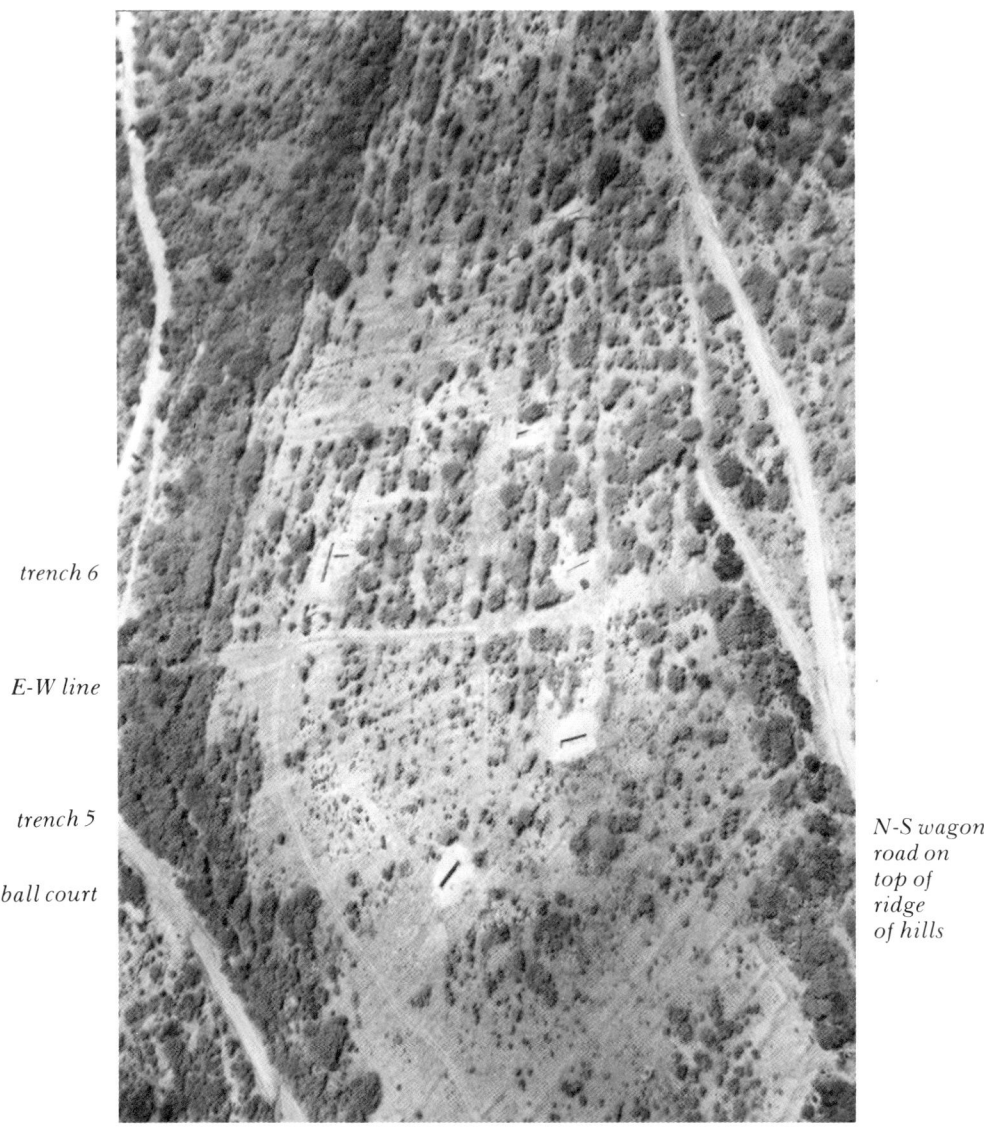

Figure 74. *Aerial photo taken by Michael Starr directly above site*

guess that the north-south lines represent dominant ploughing ridges, following the contour lines of the hillside falling eastward to the creek bed, perhaps prior to the 1967 cotton crop.

This photograph (Fig. 74) was taken from directly above the site looking southward toward the sea. Trench 5 is the most northerly excavation and the T-shaped trench 6 is the most easterly.

These were the spots where the richest artifacts were obtained—namely, the conch zemies, the ball belt fragment from trench 5, and the three whole pots, the incense burner, and the shell ornaments from trench 6.

The ball court can be seen a little to the northeast of trench 5 (just below and to the left of trench 5), and the corner stones of the court can even be seen with the aid of a hand lens. The abundance of ritual objects as well as the elegant W-O-R Saladoid pottery found in both trenches 5 and 6 suggests that this was perhaps where the shamans or chieftains lived.

I realize, in retrospect, that during my daily visits to the excavations I had become conscious of a cooler and therefore much pleasanter strip of land whenever I reached the location of trenches 5 and 6. It would be quite hot at trenches 3 and 4, but distinctly more comfortable some fifty yards eastward downhill. There seemed to be a narrow band where southerly breezes blew and I had frequently sought these desirable spots. I had puzzled over this phenomenon and suggested it might be due to the deflection of the trade winds by the ridges of hills we could see along the east and west sides of Indian Creek.

Figure 75. *Valley of Indian Creek runs horizontally across center Marmora Bay in upper part*

But it required the experience gained from Desmond's sailing the ketch Roxana into the outer and inner bays of Indian Creek (Figs. 40-46) to allow me to interpret Michael Starr's fine aerial photo (Fig. 75; also shown in color on front cover). It clearly shows the bed of Indian Creek running from left to right as a thin green band across the center of the picture. The creek is the bottom of the trough formed by two long hills marked by the thin lines of the north-south roads which mount the crests of the two flanking hills about half way to the inner bay.

It seems reasonable to suppose that those ancient bare-skinned Arawaks would have been sufficiently sensitive to temperature changes to be thoroughly aware of the favorable sea breezes being carried by this trough and deflected onto the Indian Creek site, especially at the location of trenches 5 and 6. Consequently, the strip of land that contains these trenches had been chosen as the favorite building sites, presumably by the chieftains and shamans as judged by the wealth of ritual and ornamental artifacts. Moreover, they had retained their interest in the location for several hundred years, long enough to accumulate six to ten feet of midden wastes.

January 1974

A short while before Christmas, 1973, Dr. Rouse expressed a desire not only to see the trenches that had been excavated after his illness in June, but also to examine the artifacts recovered therefrom. Arrangements were made, therefore, for a two weeks visit to the Antilles. Most of the time was spent at the Indian Creek Site and the N.A.S.A. tracking station preparing the artifacts for shipment to Yale, where they will be studied, a report prepared by Dr. Rouse, and the material returned to Antigua, retaining only an appropriate teaching collection.

I gather that the abundant yield of early Saladoid pottery is likely to give us a clearer insight into the period of occupation by the Arawaks from A.D. 400 to A.D. 900 (as indicated by the results of the first six carbon 14 dates just received). Dr. Rouse, hoping to gather information about the later periods of A.D. 1200-1500, took the opportunity of testing one of several other sites suggested by Desmond Nicholson as possibly containing later pottery—namely a location at Freeman's Bay near English Harbour. Such data may not only help to interpret the habits of the later Arawaks but might even contribute information about the highly controversial dating of the termination of Arawak occupation by the coming of the Caribs.

A three day visit was made to Martinique to compare the artifacts from Indian Creek with those displayed in the fine collections assembled in Martinique, one at the museum in Fort de France, and also the private collections of Jacques Petitjean Roget, Henri Theuvenin, and Père Pinchon.

My own impression was that in the case of the white-on-red Saladoid sherds the precision of the techniques of removing the coating of white to reveal the red coloration below was in general more meticulously practiced at Indian Creek than in the Martinique sites. On the other hand the size and variety of shapes of the bowls, some of which showed elaborately sculptured forms, were much more developed in Martinique. Likewise, the spectrum of colors was also broader and the polish of the glaze more pronounced in the Martinique pottery. I would not be surprised if these differences are explainable as local developments by a more settled and "affluent" group of people enjoying the lush environment of the well-watered expanses of fertile land. On the other hand the presence of numerous well-modeled adornos does suggest the possibility of an increasing influence by Barrancoid traders, or even invaders, whose greater concern with sculptural qualities was causing a modification of the white-on-red designs of the earlier Saladoid painters.

The consistent reference in Martinique to the large number of crudely fabricated ceramic objects in the upper occupation levels as "Carib" materials may indicate one of the major distinctions between the artifacts of Martinique and Antigua, since we have not yet found any artifacts in Antigua that we know to be of Carib fabrication.

In closing I feel obligated to record the opinion expressed by one of my Martinique friends that some of the stone pieces which I have described as "ball belt fragments" may actually be portions of broken axes. It was recommended that exact measurements be made of the surface curvatures to see if they follow the contours of an ax or a ball belt. So far I have made only contact comparison between the fragments and the available belts and axes and these visual comparisons seem to favor relation to the belts, especially when the shapes of the cross sections are considered. I must await further measurements, but will make the comment that I could learn of no "broken axes" in any of the Martinique collections that had anything like the shape of the Indian Creek fragments. Perhaps the Martinique

Arawaks were more careful of their axes and didn't break them or it just might mean that there are no ball courts in Martinique or at least that none have provided any ball belt fragments. In the meantime I feel that odds favor the ball court hypothesis for Indian Creek.

Personnel

The technical operations were under the direction of Professor Irving Rouse (Fig. 32). To carry out Dr. Rouse's program, Desmond Nicholson (Figs. 24, 39), president of the Antigua Archeological Society, was in administrative charge. Reporting to Desmond was John Meade (Figs. 9, 26), who employed and supervised all local employees: Arthur Payne (Figs. 27, 34), Binton Marsh (Fig. 76), Hilton Scott (Fig. 77), Auckland Scotland (Fig. 77), and Charlie Matthew.

In charge of the preparation of the artifacts for exhibition and study by Yale University was Elizabeth O. Kyburg (Figs. 20, 62). She was assisted by Florence Drew (Figs. 15, 62), Iris Hunt (Fig. 62), and Mildred Thomas (Fig. 62). Mary Rouse also aided in many ways.

There were also some student assistants: Dave Davis (Fig. 78), a graduate student of the Anthropology Department at Yale, who surveyed the Indian Creek site and also headed the group studying the preceramic sites at Long Island and Jolly Beach. This group comprised Margaret Wyatt, graduate anthropologist from the University of North Carolina at Chapel Hill; Hallie Whitlock (Fig. 82) of Simon's Rock, Massachusetts; Jeffrey Townsend (Fig. 83) of Locust Valley, Long Island. It is anticipated that a report on this investigation of preceramic sites will be made available in the near future. The English Harbour Yacht Club generously permitted these students to occupy their

Figure 76.
Binton Marsh

Figure 77.
Hilton Scott and Auckland Scotland

Figure 78.
Dave Davis

Figure 79.
Al Hajj Talib Dawud

Figure 80.   *Ogden Starr*

Figure 81.
Karen Gould

Figure 83.
Jeffrey Townsend and Hally Whitlock

Figure 82.
Hally Whitlock

Figure 84. *Right to left: Gregson Davis, Katie Macauley, Margo Davis and the author.*

club house, and the officers of the A.A.S. are deeply appreciative of their kindly aid.

Also assisting at the Indian Creek site was Dr. E. J. H. Boerstra, Netherlands' government archeologist in Aruba, who arrived just after Dr. Rouse went to the hospital. He supervised the technical work of preparing profiles of the trenches to establish their stratigraphy. He was also available for consultation during the last month of the excavation. Students Karen (Fig. 81) and Beckie Gould, daughters of George M. L. Gould of Mill Reef contributed ably and cheerfully to the preparation of the exhibition at the N.A.S.A. station and to other tasks.

Special recognition must be made of the continued helpfulness of Al Hajj Talib Dawud (Fig. 79), who has been unsparing of his efforts to bring about the proper understanding and preservation of the cultural and historic heritage of Antigua. He has been the effective liaison between the A.A.S. and the Antigua government officials. The president of the A.A.S., Desmond Nicholson, and the secretary-treasurer take the opportunity of expressing their gratitude for his good services.

I have stated my gratefulness to Michael Starr for permission to reproduce three of his fine aerial photographs of the site in this publication (Figs. 72, 74, 75, the latter also used in color on the front cover). Reference has also been made to his father Ogden Starr, who has contributed much to the affairs of the Antigua Archeological Society and is shown in Figure 80 examining the stratigraphy of trench 6.

It was an unexpected pleasure to receive a visit to the excavation and to the exhibition of artifacts by the distinguished Antiguan scholar Dr. Gregson Davis (Fig. 84), whom I had known many years ago as an ambitious student at the Antigua Grammar School and who sailed triumphantly through the classics course at Harvard University on a Mill Reef scholarship. He is now a professor of classics at Stanford University.

Finally, we are much appreciative of the friendly interest of those cabinet ministers and Antigua government officials who have aided us in this project, especially the Honourable Basil Peters, minister of education, health and culture, under whose sanction this excavation was conducted. The Honourable George H. Walter, premier of Antigua has consistently supported the aims and operations of the A.A.S., and we thank him for his cooperation. Also he honored us by participating in the Fifth International Congress for the Study of Pre-Columbian Cultures of the Lesser Antilles, held in St. John's, Antigua, July 22-29, 1973.